Poems from a Depressed Mind
2020 Lockdown Edition

PRETTY PUG PUBLISHING

EST. 2020

ISBN 978-1-8382149-0-6
First published in 2020 by Pretty Pug Publishing

Pretty Pug Publishing
26 The Seed Warehouse
Poole Quay BH15 1SB

SPECIAL ACKNOWLEDGMENTS

A huge thanks goes to the following people (in no particular order) who so generously donated on Kickstarter and made this dream a reality.

Stevie Dee

"No matter how hard life gets remember you are loved.
Dust yourself off and always keep fighting you're worth it."

Thank you, StevieDee x

Dianne Nicholson

"Because mental health matters."

Jason Smith

Benjamin Kitchen

Chris 'Fordie' Ford

FOREWORD
STEVE DIXON

I suffer from depression, anxiety and a mild form of temporal-lobe epilepsy.

This isn't a cry for help. It's just to explain some back story on where the idea for this book came from.

It just means my brain misfires and, has a strange way of behaving so one Saturday morning* I was up early and awake and wanted to put the words in my head onto paper. Well, onto screen.

The poems are thought provoking, funny, absolute nonsense, or whatever you want to take from them. I hope to appeal to fellow sufferers and families of who can either resonate with, or learn from what goes on in a misfiring mind!

I also hope you get a few moments of entertainment from them, as I have done writing them!

*You can see this poem on the next few pages and then what follows is whatever came into my mind!

THE ORIGINAL INSPIRATION
one Saturday morning

It's early on Saturday morning. I can't sleep
(Or more correctly, I've forgotten how to lie-in)

It's Lockdown Week 9 (but it might as well be Year 9) and I'm adhering to the
stay home message given by the government rigidly, so it angers me everyone
else that is blatantly endangering lives with their foolish actions, but this is not
the topic, for today anyway

The wind is blowing through the trees
The birds are singing
The sun is out

I sit in my comfy chair that is the perfect sun trap on these early spring mornings
I sit here alone with my thoughts
I sit some more
I go to that place - not thinking, or being

Just lost for that moment
In complete nothingness
I suffer from Depression and Anxiety

It's a battle, but not one that you might expect

I want to feel better
I convince myself I want to be better

                                                Do I want to feel better
                                                    Do I really?

I want to be off the pills
I convince myself I want to be off them
Do I want to stop taking these pills?
.. All neatly in their rows
.. In their Mon to Sun homes
That box
On the bedside table

A constant reminder
Of how I am
How I feel

                                                    Of WHO I am

---

                                            Surely no one wants this
                                                    Forever ?

Weirdly, Sometimes, I wish
.. I had a broken leg
.. or a leg missing

No, **<u>wish</u> is the wrong word**. I don't wish that on myself, or anyone. Of course
I don't
But you get my meaning when I say I wish I had something that people can see,
or understand

*This may seem a 'crazy' notion to an outsider, or those who have not
experienced it, but to those who have been or are suffering right now I think it
will resonate deeply*

*I find myself as most people do with depression and anxiety - looking at the
negatives but I feel there are so many arguments for the case against wanting
to feel better / be off the pills*

To some this is still not an illness
.. Cheer up .. Man up

If only it was that simple
.. How are you .. Are you OK?

I'm OK

Steve Dixon

Actually
I'm struggling at the moment
I'm not ok
Can I talk to you?

(Do you REALLY want to know how I am?)
(Do you REALLY want to listen?)

So back to the question
Why?
Why
would I not want to feel better?

Background: I have been on strong anti-depressants and anti-anxiety medication, for many years now

The vicious cycle
Sometimes I 'forget'
to take them

I'm feeling lazy

The Monday to Sunday boxes are empty
It's a form of self-harm

This is when you realize
You only know
When you are not on them
You crash
I crash
Life is unbearable
Life is empty
Life is impossible
Incredibly small tasks. Are impossible

I take them again
A few days later
Oh, so this is how I feel
When I am on them

Numb
Numb to the World

The numbness is like an old friend
I seek solace there
In the void
It's a weirdly comfortable place
A very comfortable place
Why would anyone want to leave?

Mindfulness
Lists of positives in my life
Things I'm grateful for
I know how they work
They don't work for me

The numbness
Is
My happy place
Is
This Normal
What is normal?

It's been so long since I felt normal
Normal?
Now I doubt
That I ever have

Perhaps
    I have to seek
        The 'New Normal'
            Isn't that what everyone is
                searching for
                    now?

And so

It's early on Saturday morning. I can't sleep
(Or more correctly, I've forgotten how to lie-in)

Not because I'm awake all night
I sleep ok now
I wake twice a night for a bladder empty
But that's just my age!

And another story

Steve Dixon

AND NOW TO THE REST...
I hope you enjoy!

THE LITERARY, JUST STUFF & NONSENSE JUKEBOX FRUIT MACHINE

I wandered lonely
I'm not proud

Ishmael lost my number
What a Moby!

[SPIDER-PIG!] [SPIDER-PIG!] [WATERMELON]

The Hills are alive!
Sadly, the Clarkes didn't make it

There's nothing, quite like, Grammar
Did you know? My Grammar' is 96 years old

Ring my
[BELL] [RING MY] [BELL]

Oranges and Lemons.
Look, enough bells please!

There is nothing like a Daim
[BAR] [BAR] [BAR]   **JACKPOT!**

AN ODE TO CUSTARD*

Yellow
Like Custard

Smooth
Like Custard

Warm
Like Custard

Bald
Like Custard

*AND HOMER SIMPSON

CAT, GET OFF MY LAPTOP!

Cat, I love you
But. Please
I'm trying to work!

Cat, I love you
I've given you fusses
I've tickled your chin
I've given you strokes
Agghh, I just can't win!

Cat, I love you
But I'm working from home
It's sunny outside
Just go out and roam

Cat, I love you
Ahhh these spreadsheets!
Cat! - go eat your treats!

Cat, I love you
I even cleaned
Your litter tray
Now, please
Just Go away!

Cat, I love you
We'll get together later
In front of the fire
Just let me finish this paper!

Cat, stop wagging that tail
I need to email!

THATS IT! CAT!, GET OFF MY LAPT-
Ewewegwheg78y3y47324!as'as;das'dlad'sldwf09wefwklrno4ntkfnro
fn3rkfnpinf-n-fkfnlkfnl3kfnlk3nglk5nt5

TO DO LIST

Get out of bed
That'll do for today
It's one better than yesterday

When I didn't get up
And stayed in my head
And tried to convince myself
I'd be better off dead

Small Steps. One at a time

Day 2 - The next day
Get Up. And,
I'll get dressed today

Small Steps. One at a time

Day 3 - The day after next
Get up. Maybe a shower - before I get dressed
I'm starting to smell a bit
And my hair is all messed

Small steps. One at a time

Not saying it's easy - I go through it too

But it's very ok
To feel this way
To have a bad day

The best thing I've found is
To talk or to write
Just let it out - I promise it will help
It all starts with
Self-help

We have to talk about it
To let it all out. Set our mind free
If just for that day, hour or second
No-one around? You can always talk to me

But we can get through this
And take it day by day

Small steps

One at a time

X

There!
Out the window

That **X**
  On the wall

Each morning
I wake

And for granted
I take

There!
Out the window

That **X**
  On the wall

Can you see?
Out the window
Behind
The Tree

There!
Out the window

That **X**
      On the wall

Where do you
Come from?

Are you a trick
Of the Sun?

There!
Out the window

That **X**
      On the wall

Like an old friend
Bringing comfort

To all

COLD BAKED BEANS

~ **FREAK!!** ~
Hot toast and butter
Cold Baked Beans

~ **FREAK!!** ~
Straight out of the tin
Cold Baked Beans

~ **FREAK!!** ~
You'll never know pleasure
Quite like Cold Baked Beans

~ **FREAK!!** ~
Here,
Try some

~ **FR-**
Oh, actually
They're quite nice

CONDIMENTS

If you look into the fridge today. You're sure of a big surprise!

If you look into the fridge today. You won't believe your eyes!

'Cause every sauce that ever there was-
Ketchup
Brown
Mayo
Sweet Chilli
Burger
Salad Cream
Pickle
Chutney
Relish
Mint
Apple
Horseradish
Mustard
Cranberry
Is there - Because Todays the day I went to Sainsburys*

other supermarkets are available

DEJA VU

Deja Vu is a nice feeling
Some say
But for me

If only you knew
What you do

Deja Vu. When you come to visit

You scare me
You haunt me

That feeling of dread
As you enter my head

It's not a pleasant visit
An uninvited
Unwanted intrusion
The feeling that surrounds me
With terror and confusion

It envelops me
Running through
My entire body
Like a swirling storm

Knowing the words people will speak
Before they say it
The things they will do

It sounds like a gift
But for me it's a nightmare
Awake but in a daze
A misty haze

I tell myself it's just my mis-wired brain
But its so tough to explain
The pain
The strain

The mental drain

I try to fight it
No, I have to fight it
Don't want to get lost in this feeling forever
When you turn up - wherever and whenever

Usually over in less that a minute
But it's far from a pleasant visit

Deja Vu - I admire your persistence
But not your existence
So please respect my sanity

And keep your distance!

FRIDAY THE 13th

Friday
The 13th
Must stay
In bed

Friday
The 13th
I'm beginning
To dread

Friday
The 13th.
The spinning
My head!

Friday
The 13th
The day
Of the dead

Oh. It's Thursday

Marvellous!

I WISH BEN STOKES WAS MY DAD

I wish Ben Stokes was my Dad

You know Ben Stokes
The Cricketer. Won the World Cup

Ben Stokes
With his strokes for four
And his pokes
To Cover

Would be a surprise
To my mother

And to my actual dad too!

I wish Ben Stokes was my Dad
Think of all the shots
He'd teach
As we play cricket
On the beach

I wish Ben Stokes was my Dad
Not just sporty
But hard too
He wouldn't mess around
With the bullies who taunted me
In the Playground

I wish Ben Stokes was my Dad
He'd pick me up from school
In his nice new car
All the other kids would drool
Cool!

My mum would ask about
My school work
You must try harder you know
But when she wasn't there
Ben Stokes would say stick-it

You're going to be The next golden boy Of cricket

I wish Ben Stokes was my Dad

You know. Ben Stokes,   **What a top bloke**

I CAN'T WAIT TO BE A GRANDAD

Because I'll be better Grandad
Than I ever was a Dad

I'll take you to the park
With seesaws, rides and swings
And get you all those Naughty things...

...Your Mum says I'm not to buy!
It won't stop me however hard they try

But as I shall proclaim out loud
I'm her Grandad so it's allowed!

I'll help you with your homework
After picking you up from school
I'll show off my mathematics skills
And, you'll think that I'm so cool!

We'll then go and play outside
In the garden if it's sunny
But if it's rainy we'll just get wet
Because it will be funny!

Steve Dixon

Granny will give you a bath
We will make such a great team
I'll make you what you want for tea
Followed by lots of ice cream!

When tea-time is over
And Granny cleans the dishes
We'll watch cartoons on the sofa
Your favourite one - with the fishes

I'll make you a hot chocolate
With marshmallows on the top
In your pink and purple mug
And blow it because its hot

So up the stairs to Bedfordshire
I'll tuck you in nice and tight
I'll read you bedtime stories
And kiss your head goodnight

*Because I'll be better Grandad
Than I ever was a Dad*

DAVE

DAVE!
He can't hear you.

DAVE!
He's not listening to you

DAVE!
He's ignoring you now

DAVE!
That's just plain rude

Try a wave

WAVE!
He can't hear a wave

WAVE! DAVE!
Oh. hello mate. Didn't see you there

And. a point. of note
My name's Richard

Oh, is it? Sorry. Dave!

HE'S FOOTBALL CRAZY [LOCKDOWN EDIT]

He's football crazy!
He's football mad!

During lockdown he learnt how to play chess,

And bake banana bread

I DON'T WANT TO GO OUT

It'll do you good
Get some fresh air
Just a five minute walk
But I don't care -

I don't want to go out

I'm happy in my comfortable space
Just sitting. Just being
I've got everything here
There's nothing outside worth seeing

I don't want to go out

I really am just happy indoors
And no I'm not being lazy
It may be tough to understand
This symptom of my crazy

I don't want to go out.

Outside are people
Who I really do dislike
So I'll stay here. With the TV
And watch something I like

I don't want to go out

It's not a permanent thing
I've told you this already
I will go out

When I'm ready

HELLO, MR PIGEON

Hello Mr Pigeon
It's very nice to meet
Have you had to come far?
I guess, from Pigeon Street

(Bet you're singing that song in your head now)

Hello Mr Pigeon
Please help yourself to seed
And take your time, there's plenty
There's no need for greed

Hello Mr Pigeon
You look so happy and content
Just sat there on my lawn
Will you be my friend?
And visit me each morn

Oh, Mr Pigeon
Where are you today?
I hope you are OK

Oh, Mr Pigeon
I missed you yesterday
And not here today
I have your favourite seed out
Please don't be far away

Hello Mr Pigeon
It's so good to have you back

I wonder
Where

you've been

I REALLY MISS TELETEXT

Ah, The good old days gone by....

LETTERS, TV GUIDES AND WEATHER!

No 24 hour programmes were to be seen
When BBC 1 finished at night
It was God Save The Queen –
And then goodnight!

ELECTION RESULTS: LABOUR BY A LANDSLIDE!

We only had three channels back in the day
Kids these days would have a breakdown
But then there were 4 - well three and a half
As channel four only started in the afternoon
With Countdown!

DID YOU EVER BUY A TELETEXT HOLIDAY?

A consonant please Carol
Now maybe a vowel
And the Mayor of Wetwang
Said, and your time starts now

THE LIVE FOOTBALL SCORES ON A SATURDAY

Simpler times, I'm talking the eighties
Grange Hill whilst eating your dinner
Bruce Forsythe on every game show
Come on down, We have a winner!

DO YOU REMEMBER THE BAMBOOZLE QUIZ?

Bonus cartoons on a Saturday morning
Blake's 7, Knight Rider, The Adventure Game
FA Cup final on BBC and ITV!
The A-Team and the kids from Fame

WAITING FOR PAGE 1 WHEN YOU'RE ON 2/100

Who knows what
TV innovations will be next
But I not really that bothered

I STILL REALLY MISS TELETEXT!

MY BEARD IS WEIRD

My beard
Is weird
It eats
More than me

My beard
Is weird
It saves me treats
For later
For my tea.

My beard
Is weird
Why does the hair
On my face
Leave a trace
All over the carpet   *(And everywhere else too)*

My beard
Is weird

But I love weird

ONLY FOOLS (AND HORSES) RUSH IN

Wise men say
Only fools and horses work

But I can't help falling in love
With you my significant other

Shall I stay? Would I be cwying?!

If I can't help falling in love with you?
You dirty little plonker!

Like a river flows
In Danger UXD

Bonjour, Bonjour, Potpourri
Some things are luvly jubbly

Take the van
Take the three wheel van

For I can't help falling in love with you
You know it makes sense!

THE COUGAR OF THE COUNTY

Looking for fun and
The ultimate bounty

Sexy
Willing
Able
That's our Mabel

She's the cougar of the county!

She likes a man in uniform
Especially a Mountie

Our Mabel will
Drink you
Under the table

She's the cougar of the county!

THE FROG KING

Arise King Charles!
Ruler of the pond

Camilla!
You look radiant
Said no-one

Arise King Charles!
The mighty amphibian

Camilla!
Oh beautiful Queen
Said no-one

Arise King Charles!
Our lily-pad leader

Camilla!
Our lady of the lake
Said no-one

Poor Camilla, but then Frogs really shouldn't marry toads!

THE LOCKDOWN BLUES

I woke up this morning

THE END

THE SIX OF HEARTS

The six of hearts lay discarded
for everyone to see

He was not alone
A diamond was there
He thought, a number three

An outcast
A freak
Not a King
Or a Queen
Or even a Jack

No lucky seven
Or ace in the pack

Be patient little six
Your time will come

When you join Four and Five
For that nice little run

TROLLS

Trolls!
Used to live under bridges
With a club demanding money

Now. They hide behind a keyboard
And think they're really funny

Trolls!
Used to live under bridges
And Demand. A Toll. To pass

Now. They live out in the cloud
With too much time. To pass

Trolls!
Used to live under bridges
Ugly, fat. And wide

Now. They are still ugly
Just on the inside.

WHERE DO BEAVERS LIVE?

Where do Beavers live?
Damn!
I've forgotten

Where do Bees live?
I've
Forgotten. Again

Where do Dolphins live?
See
I have a problem. I can't remember

Where do Bears live?
Would
You believe it. It's gone!

It's OK.
I remember now

Beavers live in America

GRATITUDE

no names
but
you know
who you are

GRATITUDE

I saved your life
Remember that
That call from your wife
To break into your flat

The worst came to mind
As I crept up the stairs
And what did I find?
The stuff of nightmares

There you lay
Naked in the bed

Floor covered in empty bottles
Discarded takeaway
And empty pill packets

I thought you were dead
Not dead, but not really with it
999 - Ambulance Please
You were taken away

This was just the beginning
The next few days
When I was by your side
Protecting you from yourself
And the outside world

For you. Your wife. Your kids
You'd taken some bad shit
I helped you through some dark times
The effect on myself didn't matter one bit

From hospital to rehab
It was an emotional few days
It's amazing in times of despair
How you go out of your ways

I would do it again
Whatever the cost to me
Do it for any
'friend'
In their hour of need

But how you treated me
When you were better
Was the worst day of my life
When you handed me that letter

Thrown well and truly
Under the biggest bus
I guess it just goes to show how
Few People you can really trust

Sealing my fate
My resignation was a formality
The wild accusations
How could you do this to me?

Misconduct, mistrust
And untruths about my motives

After everything we'd been through

I guess that's **gratitude** for you

Steve Dixon

GET IN TOUCH

I would love to hear from you.
Feedback, praise or whatever you thought!

Contact me on twitter
@stevedixonpoet

Or send an email to
steve@prettypug.co.uk

Thank-you so much for reading!
and

Look out for more
poems from a depressed mind
COMING SOON!